Anger: Defusing the Bomb

ANGER
Defusing the Bomb

Ray Burwick

Tyndale House
Publishers, Inc.
Wheaton, Illinois

Scripture references are from the King
James Version of the Bible unless
otherwise noted. Other versions used are
The Holy Bible, New International Version
(NIV) Copyright © 1978 by New York
International Bible Society; Revised
Standard Version of the Bible (RSV)
Copyright © 1952 by Division of Christian
Education of the National Council of
Churches of Christ in the United States of
America; and The Living Bible (TLB)
Copyright © 1971 by Tyndale House
Publishers.

First printing, October 1981
Library of Congress Catalog Card Number 81-50846
ISBN 0-8423-0053-8 paper
Copyright © 1981 by Ray Burwick
All rights reserved.
Printed in the United States of America

To

my family

Ann, Amy, Gretchen, and Ray II,

who have helped me to see what an angry person

I really am.

I am grateful for their patience

and love

while my reservoir of anger

continues to diminish,

thus freeing me to be the kind of husband

and father

I should and want to be.

CONTENTS

PREFACE

Anger is not the cause of all personality problems. As you read this material, you might begin to wonder if dandruff or falling hair might not be linked to pent-up anger. (It might be!)

I am the first to admit that there are definitely other causes for mental, emotional, physical, social, and spiritual dysfunction. Other counselors may disagree, I know, but from my own experience in counseling, pent-up anger causes these conflicts more than any other single factor. As I see clients resolve their resentments, I see them become free to be whole and happy.

This book is written mainly for people who want to include the spiritual dimension in their personal growth. Many people are turned off to the church and religion, but I find very few true atheists. God can not only give us insights into our angry natures, but can give us the power to change what we, in our own strength, couldn't change about ourselves.

I trust that this material will bring to us a deeper sense of freedom so that we may experience all that our Creator has in mind for us.

As I sit at the typewriter in my office, I view the couch from which many angry people have poured out their stories. "The wise man seeks counsel." Some leave the office convinced that circumstances must dictate how they react: "If HE will change, then I will be okay," some of them say. Their lives continue to be torn and tossed about by circumstances as they hang onto that condition for recovery.

Others leave the office with a commitment to accept personal responsibility. They say to themselves, "Sure, I've been wronged. It hurts. I'm very resentful because of it. But I can change."

Like a flower, the blossom opens and a deep beauty emerges from the previous hard shell of hurt and resentment. They are free—free to experience an abundant life-style not determined by circumstances. I sincerely wish this kind of freedom for everyone who hurts.

ACKNOWLEDGMENTS

I owe much gratitude to Bonnie
(Mrs. William) Bailey, who encouraged me
to put in writing the material I was
presenting to groups. She even supported
her encouragement by offering to do the
bulk of the typing. Thanks, Bonnie.

Constructive criticism was sought from
my wife, Ann, from Dan Allison, Frank
Barker, Dr. William Bailey, Dr. Jack
Taylor, Clarke Stallworth, Dr. Charles
Solomon, and from Dr. Henry Brandt.
I am grateful for their critique.

Sharon Boyd and my wife also helped in
typing preliminary drafts. Thank you.

The delightful cartoon ideas are from
Shirley (Mrs. George) Dye.

To the scores of authors from whom
I have learned much, I am grateful.

Finally, I want to express my thanks
to my clients for sharing themselves with

me so that we together have learned much about defusing our bombs. The cases I have presented in this material are either camouflaged to protect confidentiality, or permission has been granted to present the facts.

The size of a man
is measured
by what makes him angry.

ONE
The Hidden Bomb
A Definition of Anger

A tall, fifteen-year-old boy, well mannered but shy, stood in front of his grandmother and calmly shot her to death. He was quoted as saying, "I just wondered how it would feel to shoot Grandmother."

A kindly silver-haired gentleman of seventy-eight sat in my counseling office and said, "Ray, I've put up with my wife's criticism all these years and I just can't take it any longer. I want a divorce."

"Dr. Burwick, can you tell me why I have these chest pains? I've been thoroughly checked out medically. Physicians can't find any organic cause for the pain. They say it is caused by tension. Can you help me?" another patient asked.

Other counselors may have different

experiences, but it is some form of anger—irritations, frustrations, resentment, bitterness, hate—that brings more people to my counseling office than any other factor. As in the three cases mentioned, most of them do not realize their anger is as devastating as it is. Much of anger is hidden.

Explosive anger is "harmful to your health," as the warning labels read. But hidden or unrecognized anger is by far the most devastating kind, causing most symptoms physically, such as ulcers, high blood pressure, and migraines. Spiritual symptoms are lack of inner peace and joy. Emotionally, anger causes anxiety and depression. Mentally, it can cause confused thinking—even insanity.

As the Swiss psychiatrist Paul Tournier stated, "Violence is in the heart of all men, but we all have an inbuilt resistance to recognizing it as a thing that concerns us."

Every Christian ought to ask himself: "Does this apply to me? Can I see myself? Am I an angry person?"

ANGER DEFINED

Anger is defined as "the energy we experience when an obstacle is confronted in the process of need-fulfillment." For

Just teed off

example, a need or expectation is not being met and because of this frustration, we can experience feelings of extreme hostility or simply a kind of indignation. Anger is often a person's condemning judgment, a usurpation of God's role as judge.

Considering these definitions of anger, we may ask, "Why is my blood pressure so high?" "Why do I lose my temper?" "Why do I feel like I am burning up inside?" To understand, we may begin by examining how anger develops.

GROWTH OF ANGER

We are born angry. Freud had no conflict with the Bible when he said: "Man is born basically evil." "We started out bad, being born with evil natures, and were under God's anger" (Eph. 2:3, TLB).

A few years ago, when I was disciplining one of our children for disobedience, she said, "Daddy, if Adam hadn't sinned, I wouldn't be in trouble now!"

We realize that our children have to be taught wholesome attitudes and behavior, and, as they obey God, he makes them "good." We don't have to teach them to be "bad." That comes naturally. Our bent to self-centeredness, starting at birth, underlies most of our anger.

Anger develops naturally, as we can learn from observing a baby when it doesn't get its way. One of our friends has an infant son who doesn't like to lie on his stomach. His father will place him in that position and the place becomes bedlam. The baby kicks and squirms, his face gets red, and he becomes furious because he cannot get over onto his back.

Such behavior is normal for a child, but very often childish temper tantrums evolve into adults' sophisticated anger, which we call pity-parties or depression.

Anger is learned. "Keep away from angry, short-tempered men lest you learn to be like them" (Prov. 22:24, 25, TLB). Recently I had a deluge of child-raising problems appear in my counseling practice. Each of these teenagers was a very angry person.

In nearly every situation, there was at least one parent who was also a very angry person. Since anger was not resolved, it was being modeled to, and learned by, the children.

Do children have the right to say to their

parent or parents, "I'm angry because I'm just like you?"

Self-esteem affects anger. The more self-absorbed a person is, the greater his or her needs appear to be. The process begins, for example, when a man doesn't have a very good self-image. As a result, he becomes more aware of himself, aware of how circumstances affect him. If things don't go his way, he becomes fearful and threatened, perhaps even envious or hurt, all of which lead directly to anger. If the anger isn't resolved, it begins to poison him and contaminate all those around him.

Anger is not a problem of a few people. Most of us carry around a weight of unresolved anger, reaching all the way back into childhood, whether we are aware of it or not.

Some psychological theories differ with these views of anger. There is a belief that anger is a biological phenomenon built into the gene structure. According to this view, aggression must be released through culturally acceptable outlets, or brain surgery must be performed, or chemicals such as Valium to reduce hostility must be taken, or electrodes must be implanted under the scalp to receive hostility-reducing amounts of electricity.

ANGER DISTORTION
Buried anger. "I never get angry," he said. Robert, a meticulously dressed middle-aged man sat in my office, facing not only a possible divorce but the criminal charge of attempted murder.

"What do you mean?" I asked. "Everyone gets angry at times."

"Not me," he replied.

Robert's wife, Shirley, had been driving because Robert had become too intoxicated again. Shirley had criticized him for drinking and the tank exploded—Robert's, that is. He pulled a revolver out of the glove compartment and shot at her. Fortunately, in his drunken stupor he had missed.

Robert is an example of an anger distortion called *burial,* which is an unconscious denial or nonadmittance of anger; the stuffing of anger into the subconscious mind.

The repressed person, who buries his anger, may say that he never gets angry. Either this person is a liar, has a poor memory, lives a very dull life, is first in line for the first vacancy in the Trinity, or is deceiving himself. Anger is a natural emotion which everyone experiences.

Canned Anger. A similar distortion of anger is *canning* it. "Yes sir, since I've become a Christian, I'd like to report to you that I've completely controlled my temper. I still get angry, but no one else knows about it. I keep it inside," such a person claims.

A person who is canning anger shoves it within, sits on it, covers it over, masks it, and soon may not even be aware of it. Canned anger is often characterized by "I just put it out of my mind. I try to forget it. I take a pill or a shot of whiskey. I just laugh it off. No one is going to control me."

But the reservoir of anger builds, and the accumulated poison becomes more and more potent. Canned hostility is not necessarily hostility conquered. Hostility can be a very silent, sleeping giant, but the slightest provocation will bring it forth in all its ugliness. Like the lava trapped in the Mt. St. Helens volcano, it has to flow. Thus the person who *buries* anger says, "I am not aware of anger," while one with *canned* anger says, "I'm aware of anger, but I'll keep it within me."

Transference

Transference. The third distortion is misplaced anger or *transference.* Sometimes we remove anger from the directed source because, for some reason, we are too threatened to admit the fact that we are angry at the boss, at our spouse, or at God. We transfer the anger to a less threatening source or situation.

Transference is depicted by the man who gets angry at his boss but cannot resolve it. If he spewed out anger at work, or tried to confront his boss, he might get fired. So he takes that anger home with him and transfers it to his wife with comments like, "Why isn't dinner ready? I thought we were going to have roast duck, but I see it's burnt offering!" The wife receives the brunt of the man's anger. She becomes angry.

Transference may continue. Instead of resolving it within herself and with him, she then lashes out at the child. The child, not able to resolve anger because he or she does not see parents working through and resolving anger, then kicks the dog. The dog bites the cat, and the cat goes to the backyard and chases a chipmunk. On and on we go. Transference does not resolve anger, but transfers it to some other object.

Camouflage. The fourth distortion of anger is *camouflage.* There is a barrier or a wall between thinking and feeling. Feelings are masked. Paul Tournier in his book *Violence Within* (New York: Harper and Row, 1978) describes it as internal and external languages:

> But when the gulf is widened between the internal and external languages, like the two banks of a river becoming further apart, it becomes impossible eventually to bridge the gap, and the result is a state of anxiety, a sign of rupture in the unity of the person. The psychotherapist's consulting room, with its exceptional climate of truth, is the place where a bridge can be built joining the two sides together again, so that the patient may at last become his real self.

It seems that the more intelligent my clients are, the more they tend to camouflage their anger. A brilliant young physician sat in my counseling office. His psychiatrist had told him that shock treatments were the only way to bring him out of his depression.

"Ray, there is no way I can have shock treatments. My practice would be ruined."

Surgery and his brilliant mind had been his life. A rejecting wife, some professional criticism, childhood hurts, and rejections had led Sam to a deep-seated resentment that had smouldered within him for years. It had found its outlet through depression so profound that he was at the point of taking his life.

When we would talk about these irritations and frustrations, Sam was quick to make comments like, "But, I love her," or "My parents did their best," or "He couldn't help it," or "But look how bad I was in that situation."

Instead of looking at the feelings of hurt, resentment, bitterness, and even hate, Sam would quickly intellectualize the circumstances. Feelings were not surfaced and resolved. Anger was being camouflaged.

One of the most frequent camouflages I see in counseling is "I was hurt." Anyone who uses that phrase is probably a very angry person, because the word "hurt" is a blanket that often covers a bed of anger. If you are feeling only hurt, you may not be in touch with your anger.

Other phrases I hear that camouflage anger are, "I'm a Christian, so I forgive." But all the evidence shows the person is still angry. "I'm not angry. My voice is just loud because I'm excited. Besides, only fools get angry."

GROWTH OF ANGER DISTORTION

Anger distortion has a beginning. We should learn how we express and resolve our anger.

Childhood stifling. Distortions begin in childhood when children are taught to stifle anger. Parents have told children not to get angry with them. Or perhaps parents told children not to hold in anger, but have threatened them with such remarks as "Let it out, but I will knock your block off if you are disrespectful!"

In my estimation, a healthy home climate is one of openness where children are allowed to tell parents of their anger toward them. I think that there is a dishonoring way of expressing anger, and we cannot let our children do that. If they are attacking us, verbally or physically, or calling us names, or if they are expressing their hate in a disrespectful way, we cannot allow it.

Distortion is also demonstrated to the child by the stoic, or nonfeeling, parent who says, "It's crazy to get angry. What

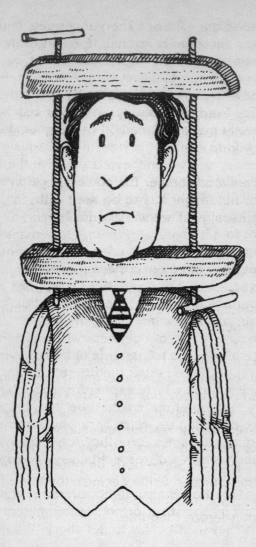

I was under pressure

good does it do?" Then anger gets buried, and the child is not taught how to express or resolve anger in a constructive way.

It is important that we teach children how to express what is going on inside. For example: "Daddy, what you just did really made me mad." I can encourage the child to explain his view. I then explain mine, and we endeavor to resolve the conflict. Whether the conflict is resolved or not, anger has to be dealt with biblically, as we will discuss later.

HINDRANCES TO
EXPRESSION AND RESOLUTION
As we grow to adulthood, there are hindrances to expressing and resolving anger.

Fear. Some of us must face the fact that if we really saw what is going on within us, we would see murder. "Am I a monster?" we would ask ourselves. In fact, we have even let our real feelings surface occasionally enough to say, "I'd like to kill that guy!" Some of us do not like to face the monster within because there is a fear that we might actually succumb to the murderous thoughts.

"Nice guy" syndrome. Anger resolution is hindered by our trying to be a nice guy, so we feel we have to cover up the anger.

Emotional isolation. Some isolate themselves emotionally, like the person who says, "I won't get involved. I have been hurt enough." In order not to be hurt any more, such a person builds walls around himself. Consequently, with no involvement, there is no cause for anger to flare up. All the hurt, however, that began building those walls, is covering a reservoir of unresolved anger.

Insecurity. Others say, "I *must* be in control. I *must* control!" The opinions of others are considered so important and since people admire a controlled person, the insecure person is hindered from resolving his or her anger.

Insecurity might also be manifested in an inability to confront. Very often a wife feels like a doormat. She has been taught to submit to her husband. It is the insecure woman who not only submits, but may also become subservient, too insecure to confront; and in her dishonesty she becomes a very angry doormat at that. Her insecurity breeds a fear of rejection. "If

I tell my husband that I'm angry about what is going on, or if I tell him that he isn't fair, he might reject me. He might even leave me."

Distorted Christianity. Another hindrance to expressing and resolving anger is a distorted idea about Christianity. Some say, "Christians don't get angry, so I can't be angry. It's a sin to be angry, so I'm not angry. I'm upset."

As one minister said to me, "Ray, am *I* exercised!" He felt if he were angry, he would be sinning and he could not stand the fact that there might be any sin in his life.

Such a distorted idea makes one become overly concerned for his reputation. "What would people think if they saw me angry?" For some, recognizing what they are doing to avoid facing their anger is enough to help them resolve it properly. Others must suffer some of the effects of it before they are motivated to seek better solutions.

TWO
What the Bomb Can Do
The Results of Anger

A considerable amount of poison results from unresolved anger. From my counseling practice and from my own personal experience, it seems as if unresolved anger is the underlying cause of nearly everything wrong with us—from ingrown toenails to dandruff!

Obviously, I am being facetious. Fear, worry, insecurity, virus, birth defects, biochemical imbalance, drug abuse—all of these can cause disease. But as I see my clients resolving their anger problems, I observe a significant lessening of symptoms, more than with any other kind of resolution. Most depression ceases, anxiety diminishes, migraines, stomach and intestinal disorders and a host of other

complaints become less intense or no
problem at all.

DEATH

With psychiatrists Minirth and Meier in
Happiness Is a Choice (Grand Rapids:
Baker, 1978) I believe anger is probably
the leading cause of death. It is amazing
what anger does to us! The Bible tells us
about it in several places. "And by all
means don't brag about being wise and
good if you are bitter and jealous and
selfish; that is the worst sort of lie. For
jealousy and selfishness are not God's
kind of wisdom. Such things are earthly,
unspiritual, inspired by the devil. For
wherever there is jealousy or selfish
ambition, there will be disorder and every
other kind of evil" (James 3:14-16, TLB).
Every other kind of evil!

   While I was writing this book, a friend
told me that his father was so angry he
had choked to death. In checking this
with an internist, I was told that anger can
induce a vomiting episode that can
cause aspiration.

BITTERNESS

"Watch out that no bitterness takes root
among you, for as it springs up it causes

deep trouble" (Heb. 12:15, TLB). The reservoir or accumulation of anger within us might be lying dormant, but very often it activates into grotesque poisonous shapes, not recognizable as anger. If we are not resolving anger within us, we are controlling it, or burying it, or stifling it; consequently, we do the same to our positive emotions.

One exciting aspect of my counseling practice is to watch people become more loving as they begin to resolve anger. As they are freeing themselves up from the controls of anger, they are also releasing the ability to be able to express more love, care, and tenderness toward others.

S. I. McMillen, a physician skillful in writing as well as in practicing medicine, speaks of the devastating effect of hatred. In *None of These Diseases* (Westwood, NJ: Revell, 1963), he wrote:

The moment I start hating a man, I become his slave. I can't enjoy my work any more because he even controls my thoughts. My resentments produce too many stress hormones in my body and I become fatigued after only a few hours of work. The work I formerly enjoyed is now drudgery. Even

I was fed up

vacations cease to give me pleasure. It may be a luxurious car that I drive along a lake fringed with the autumn beauty of maple, oak, and birch. As far as my experience of pleasure is concerned, I might as well be driving a wagon in mud and rain.

The man I hate hounds me wherever I go. I can't escape his tyrannical grasp on my mind. When the waiter serves me porterhouse steak with french fries, asparagus, crisp salad, and strawberry shortcake smothered with ice cream, it might as well be stale bread and water. My teeth chew the food and I swallow it, but the man I hate will not permit me to enjoy it.

The man I hate may be miles from my bedroom; but more cruel than any slave driver, he whips my thoughts into such a frenzy that my innerspring mattress becomes a rack of torture. The lowliest of serfs can sleep, but not I. I really must acknowledge the fact that I am a slave to every man on whom I pour the vials of my wrath.

ANXIETY

A young lady sat in my office, shaking. She was not afraid, not sick, not cold.

She was angry. Having talked with her previously, I knew that her missionary parents had trained her well to bury all negative feelings: "Anger is not Christlike—stifle it." When she had been sent to missionary boarding school at a young age, she perceived this forced separation as rejection.

"Mom and Dad had time for everyone but me. They even shipped me off to boarding school when I was seven."

Rejection and bitterness, buried, began to grow. She was married at the time she came to see me. Her husband was very passive and she had to make all the decisions. She had to run the household. His philosophy, like many men, was "I bring home the bacon. You prepare it."

There was no sharing. There was very little unity. He wasn't sensitive to her emotional needs. Rejection, again and again. More bitterness—buried. And there she sat, shaking like a leaf.

I had a towel in my desk. I folded it, gave it to her, and said, "This towel represents your husband's neck."

Before she could even think of what was happening, she was wringing that towel with all her strength. A couple of seconds later she realized the dynamics of her action and said, "Ray, I didn't realize how much I hated Jim." Her shaking stopped immediately and she began the process of resolving the angry spirit she had been carrying for years. Anger is the blood brother of anxiety.

PERSONALITY DISORDERS

Anger can cause personality disorders like the very rigid person who says, "No" to everything. Recently, a father in New York was murdered because of his two children, ages ten and twelve. The two hired a professional killer for fifty dollars to do away with him. Why? The children indicated: "All Dad said was 'No' to everything we asked of him. We couldn't take it any more."

Anger is sometimes exposed through sarcasm, bitter words, and saccharine sweetness. The one who is outwardly very, very sweet is often one with much pent-up anger.

DEPRESSION

Anger causes stilted behavior and most depression. The first thing we need to ask about our depression is "Am I angry at someone?" Unresolved anger is the underlying cause of most depression and self-pity.

MENTAL PROBLEMS

Most mental symptoms are caused by pent-up anger—obsessive compulsions, phobias, fantasies, and schizophrenia. When a person comes into my office with these kinds of symptoms, talking weirdly of hearing bells or voices, I say, "I'm sure it seems real, but it is not. That is crazy talk. We're wasting your time. Let's talk about the cause." The underlying cause is almost always unresolved anger, and as it is dealt with, the mental symptoms begin to fade.

Sometimes emotional or mental healing can be very quick. It does not have to be a long process. The writer of Hebrews said, "The word of God is quick, and powerful, and sharper than any two edged sword, piercing even to the dividing asunder of soul and spirit" (Heb. 4:12). A person who really wants to be free from mental disorders can change rather quickly. God is "a rewarder of them that diligently seek him" (Heb. 11:6). However, let us remember that life-styles aren't changed overnight.

GUILT

Anger can underlie guilt which causes food-related symptoms, as eating too much or too little. The latter is the person who refuses to eat or who eats and then induces vomiting until he or she becomes thinner and thinner. One person who started at 130 pounds finally died of starvation at the weight of sixty pounds. The anger within was not faced, was not resolved, which caused guilt feelings. The subconscious reasoning continued that the guilt had to be punished, and punishment could be either overeating or undereating or even starvation.

Anorexia nervosa is the medical term for a pathological loss of appetite for psychic reasons accompanied usually by emaciation and sometimes death by starvation.

Sharon was a highly intelligent, articulate seventeen-year-old, who nearly died at half her normal body weight. Some time after her stay in the intensive care unit to treat the anorexia nervosa, we met and began to penetrate the walls of insecurity and masked bitterness that had been built around this lovely girl. Weeks lapsed into months, forced feedings, hospitalizations, some temporary breakthroughs in counseling, but always an underlying stubbornness, rebellion, and manipulation.

To illustrate, Sharon's physician had her on a two-pounds-per-week weight gain plan that "frosted the cake." After a few weeks, the doctor noticed she was getting thinner and thinner, yet the scales indicated a gain of two pounds per week. On that fateful day of discovery, she was asked to strip before the weigh-in. Sewn to her slip were eighteen pounds of railroad spikes. Many other similar escapades led to that one Saturday morning when she finally saw that she was missing out on life. She began to resolve the inner dynamics of which anger was a part, and has been gaining weight and now is growing into a delightful, well-adjusted person.

CONVERSION HYSTERIAS

Many sleep-related problems are caused by unresolved anger as *conversion hysterias,* which could be, for instance, a temporary blindness, or loss of speech, or paralysis of an arm or leg with no medical explanation. A man's anger toward his wife was grotesque and deep, and it had never been resolved. Out of the blue one day he had an urge to pick up a knife and stab her. Instead of facing what was going on inside, an unconscious reaction paralyzed the arm he would have used to stab her. This paralysis was a classic example of conversion hysteria.

ACCIDENT PRONENESS
Anger held in often results in subconscious self-punishment as in the careless use of knives, guns, machinery, or automobiles. A clumsy, accident-prone person may really be an angry person.

WORKAHOLISM
The overindulgent person is often one who escapes resolving anger through work, sports, and other activities. When a person is always busy, he doesn't have to stop and face what might be happening inside.

AGGRESSION
The angry person can be an aggressive identifier such as the owner of a huge, vicious dog; or a little old lady viewing a wrestling match from the front row yelling, "Kill him!"

Dr. Theodore Rubin's *Angry Book* (New York: Macmillan, 1969), does an excellent job of explaining the psychosomatic dynamics of anger. Briefly, he says:

The ears receive soundwaves; the eyes receive lightwaves that convey messages to the brain in which is integrated information that makes us angry. This feeling is felt by the entire body. Messages are sent out by chemical changes in nerves so that various hormones are excreted: heart-rate changes, the diameter of blood vessels change, and so on. These effects in turn affect the skin, musculature, the digestive tract, the lungs—all the systems and organs of the body. Messages that are smooth and free-flowing will see healthy expression; messages that are polluted will have poisonous physical repercussions.

PSYCHOSOMATIC ILLNESS

A psychosomatic illness is still an illness! A stomach ulcer hurts! If there is a perforation, the person is in trouble. But the cause is very often anger. A medication, such as Tagamet, may be used for that stomach ulcer, and sometimes surgery is necessary, but the underlying cause must be resolved or there will continue to be other psychosomatic problems.

It is amazing how often migraines are taken care of by a good, quick, temper tantrum. Many asthmatics experience relief as they learn to cry. Beethoven is thought to have brought on his own deafness by a fit of temper.

The following information from a mental health journal is frightening. It states that doctors are warning people who grimly suppress their emotions, and people who vent every emotion, are more likely to end up with cancer than people who are moderate but consistent in expressing how they honestly feel. In other words, both extremes of burying everything or venting everything can be equally dangerous.

Anger appears to be one of the precipitating causes of arthritis. A beautiful young woman sat in my office with the twisted, swollen joints of rheumatoid arthritis. It had begun two years previously, when she became a Christian. The tremendously volatile temper she had carried as a teenager was not in keeping with her view of what a Christian ought to be, so she buried the temper. Within weeks arthritis began. Another woman I saw was normal until she caught her husband in bed with another woman.

Her arthritis flared so fast that she was in a wheelchair within thirty days.

OTHER SYMPTOMS

Other symptoms of anger can be *elephant mind* ("Do you remember twenty-five years ago on our honeymoon when you watched TV instead of celebrating our marriage?"); *giggling* at the wrong time; *chronic forgetting; talking out loud* during movies and plays; *bumping into people; habitual lateness; embarrassing a companion; giving misinformation;* or a sudden attack of *stupidity*.

Very subtle symptoms often appear, such as the "Don't worry about me" manipulation. This is typified by the parent who has a hard time cutting the apron strings, and says, "Sure, you can go out on a date. Don't worry about me, even though I might be dead by the time you get back."

The malicious gossip is an angry person. Dreams of violence and death, or fantasies of violence or death are anger symptoms, as is chronic, malicious joking.

Others who may be angry are the "peace-keepers," who never say a harsh word, the sexually provocative, perhaps

I blew up

trying to get even with a mate, the energy-drained person who says, "I just don't have energy for anything."

The person who retreats or withdraws, the intolerant person, the pessimist—any of these may be an angry person. The person with much distrust, the one who is seldom pleased, the person with no joy, the bore, the person who uses drugs, the maniac driver, or the teeth grinder.

One of my angry clients shared his teeth-grinding experience. He had, over the past ten years, developed two stress-related physiological problems resulting in surgery. Over the years, because of unresolved emotional problems, it became a habit for him to clench his teeth. The repeated hard bite possibly triggered growth of additional bone about the upper and lower jaw in an effort to help the jaw to sustain the added forces. Also, the teeth, especially in the front of the mouth, were worn down so much that a special retainer had to be made to prevent him from clenching his teeth.

The strain, due to the oversized jaw, caused the gums to pull away from the teeth, and peridontal disease, an infection of the gum tissue, developed. Toxins from the infection were carried away by the blood supply to the infected tissue, and these toxins in the blood reduced his body health in general.

The doctors thought that these problems, especially the bone growth, was either congenital, or the results of ongoing stress, and in his case, the latter seemed more plausible. The gum disease was hastened by inconsistent dental preventive maintenance, such as brushing and flossing of the teeth, during periods of prolonged depression. In short, the man was literally destroying himself.

The third leading cause of teenage death is suicide. In most cases, suicide is the ultimate expression of anger. "When I am gone, you'll be sorry. You'll pay. You caused my death, and you will know it!"

One man left a death note that read: "I love my God. I love my country. I love my children; but my wife is a bitch." A policeman saw him blow his brains out. I counseled the remains of his wife.

John Hunter (1728-1793), an English physician, developed angina pectoris (chest pains caused by deficient oxygenation of the heart muscles) and was one of the first to describe the symptoms. He has been quoted as saying, "My life is in the hands of any rascal who chooses to annoy and tease me." Violent disagreements with his colleagues that brought on the chest pains hastened his death and a heart attack finally ended his life.

Murder is an obvious result of anger. One research indicated that 90 percent of the murderers studied grew up with a father who was absent, brutal, alcoholic, or else so passive and demeaned as to command no respect.

Anger produces more immediate effects on the body's chemical balance than any other emotion, and while the feeling may pass quickly, the damage, like a hurricane, is devastating.

There can be other causes for all the above symptoms, but pent-up anger is probably the leading cause of disease and death. Some chiropractors say, "If you're sick, you're out of adjustment." Some nutritionists say, "If you are sick, you are not eating right." Let us not be as dogmatic, but we should ask, "Is my malady caused by my pent-up anger?"

THREE
Defusing the Bomb
The Remedy
for Anger

Dr. Henry Brandt says "We live in an angry society." Most of us, maybe all, have some unresolved anger within us. It is important that we know how to resolve it.

If I could invent a pill that would dissolve all anger, I could retire a millionaire tonight. Billions of dollars are spent yearly on medical bills, on counseling, on medications, while much of the illness being treated is caused by pent-up anger.

GET RID OF ANGER
How do we deal with anger? What is the remedy? Because the Bible professes to be the guide to successful living, we must examine what it says about anger.

"It is better to be slow-tempered than famous" (Prov. 16:32, TLB).

"Don't be quick-tempered—that is being a fool" (Eccles. 7:9, TLB).

"It is best to listen much, speak little, and not become angry; for anger doesn't make us good, as God demands that we must be" (James 1:19, 20, TLB).

I can relate to the first two: "Listen much, speak little." Until the age of twenty-eight, I stuttered profusely. Consequently, I spoke little and listened much. But as I was listening much and speaking little, a large reservoir of anger was building inside me. I have had the challenge of letting the Lord clean out that anger which had helped trigger the stuttering along with some other painful symptoms.

The Bible also says, "Get rid of your feelings of hatred" (1 Peter 2:1, TLB). "Now is the time to cast off and throw away all these rotten garments of anger, hatred, cursing, and dirty language" (Col. 3:8, TLB).

BE AWARE OF ANGER—STEP ONE
The psalmist was concerned about his anger. "Search me, O God, and know

my heart: try me, and know my thoughts: and see if there be any wicked way in me, and lead me in the way everlasting" (Ps. 139:23, 24). "Cleanse thou me from secret faults. Keep back thy servant also from presumptuous sins" (Ps. 19:12, 13), he prayed in another place. We may try to cover these attitudinal sins. But God often reveals them to us, especially our anger, through dreams, reading of Scripture, prayer, confrontation with another person, and in other reactions with people.

Most of us don't like to admit that we could be angry. Sometimes it is very hard to pray the psalmist's "awareness prayer." Even when we do, it is still difficult to say, "Yes, I own my anger." We would rather rationalize or defend ourselves. "If my wife just wouldn't cram the toothpaste tube, I wouldn't get angry," we say, still blaming the cause on others.

R. D. Palmer surveyed more than 500 hospitalized psychiatric and nonpsychiatric patients. He found that the feature most characteristic of the group was conflict involving fear and inhibition (holding in) about angry feelings. These were people who wanted to lash out at others but felt guilty or anxious about their anger. Dr. Palmer saw these people not so much as being constantly filled with boiling anger. Rather, they were people easily provoked. When stirred up, they became anxious and tense with internal conflict, but still often denying the anger within them.

The first step to defusing the anger bomb is to be aware and accept how angry we really are.

EXPRESS IT—STEP TWO
Once we allow God to bring to the surface our angry spirits, expression must take place. Some would suggest the angry person beat a pillow. Others tell him to scream. Some say, "Imagine the person with whom you are angry sitting at a banquet nude, eating with his fingers." Others suggest telephoning the person with whom he is angry and chewing him out, but keeping the finger on the cradle of the phone. Others suggest writing a letter expressing all the hate but not mailing the letter.

The Arabs have discovered the camel has a great ability for hatred. If the camel thinks the driver has mistreated it, it will bide its time before hurting the driver, but sooner or later it will retaliate. Anticipating this, the driver places his clothes in a conspicuous place, in the form of a sleeping man. When the camel sees the clothes, it tramples them viciously. The driver is then free of fear. The camel's rage has been vented.

How often do we also, in a fit of blind rage, have difficulty distinguishing between the real and the unreal—the fact and prejudice?

Among medical and psychological clinicians, there is a wide variance of philosophy regarding anger ventilation. Scream therapists place people on the floor and teach them how to kick, beat, and scream, triggering past memories. As they see those memories, they scream out, freeing themselves from blockage. Hundreds of people are paying thousands of dollars for the treatment.

A California psychologist was sued recently for a technique he called rage reduction. His theory was described by the claimant: "I was tortured, including choking, beating, which included holding and tying me down and sticking fingers in my mouth."

Most counseling professionals believe that ventilative therapies ("Get your anger out") can have positive results in treating anger-producing conflicts. As a person is encouraged to vent his feelings, his anxiety is reduced. The person learns that he isn't going to be punished for showing his resentment. He can admit to himself that anger does reside within him and not be bothered by the awareness. If the person is a Christian, he then can treat the anger biblically.

Though I believe anger needs to be expressed, it is not necessary to act out one's hostility. Angry feelings can be discussed and described without attacking others verbally or physically.

Some ventilationists encourage indiscriminate expression of anger in the counseling office—such as sticking pins into dolls—believing anger will be kept in proper bounds if dealt with clinically. But violence has a way of getting out of hand and can breed further violence. And, some people need stronger restraints to their anger. Their quick tempers have spread devastation.

Leonard Berkowitz, writing in *Psychology Today,* stated: "The evidence dictates now that it is unintelligent to encourage persons to be aggressive, even if, with the best of intentions, we want to limit such behavior to the confines of psychotherapy."

I lost my head

The extreme view of nonexpression of anger is typified by Dr. Milton Laden, who, as a member of the Psychiatric Department of Johns Hopkins Medical School stated: "Don't express anger. It is contagious, and as you express it, it returns back to you."

How do you resolve these conflicting views of anger expression? Biblically, we look at David, a "man after God's own heart." Notice how David expressed anger:

Show him how it feels! Let lies be told about him, and bring him to court before an unfair judge. When his case is called for judgment, let him be pronounced guilty. Count his prayers as sins. Let his years be few and brief; let others step forward to replace him. May his children become fatherless and his wife a widow; may they be evicted from the ruins of their home. May creditors seize his entire estate and strangers take all he has earned. Let no one be kind to him; let no one pity his fatherless children. May they die. May his family name be blotted out in a single generation. Punish the sins of his father and mother. Don't overlook them. Think constantly about the evil things he has done, and cut off his name from the memory of man. [Ps. 109:6-15, TLB]

David wrote: "O God . . . why have you forsaken me?" (Ps. 42:9, TLB). I don't think David was saying this sweetly and softly. He was making an expression of deep anger. If we are angry because someone pulls in front of us to get a parking space, this is not deep anger that justifies our calling out to God, "Why have you forsaken me?" Losing a parking place is such a minor irritation we should be able to say, "Okay, God, I blew this one. I'm angry. I see it. Forgive me."

CONFESS IT—THE ULTIMATE EXPRESSION OF ANGER

It is my opinion that if anger is not expressed, it stays within us, contaminating us. The best expression of anger is to God in the form of confession. "Lord, I'm really ticked off. Forgive me. Help me focus on resolving my part of the problem instead of pointing the finger at the other person." Christ came not to encourage us to ventilate anger but to free us from it.

"But," you say, "what if I've just found

that my spouse is having an affair? You expect me to confess my anger when it is my partner who is in bed with another person? You're crazy. They are the ones who need to be confessing."

That is true. That is what *they* should do. Their adulterous relationship is certainly sin. But if *we* hang onto an angry response, causing ourselves depression, anxiety, and other physical complaints, we are reacting sinfully also. We are responsible for our reactions. "If we confess our sins, he is faithful and just to forgive . . . and to cleanse" (1 John 1:9).

"God, that spouse of mine is being unfaithful. That's wrong. That hurts. I'm feeling like a zero. I'm angry. But God, take my angry spirit." If our reaction of anger isn't resolved, it will destroy us.

Sometimes in marriage we can be so angry at our spouse that we won't even pray that way. We should pray, "God, make me willing to face my anger. Make me willing to face *my* sin, because right now I would rather point the finger. Make me willing to accept my responsibility for the problem."

Some people would call that kind of prayer a cop-out. "God won't do what you can do for yourself," they insist. I believe we can be hurt so deeply that all the human strength we can muster to activate our wills to forgive the unforgivable is not enough. There are times when we need to apply Paul's promise: "God is at work within you, helping you want to obey him, and then helping you do what he wants" (Phil. 2:13, TLB).

There are times I don't want to obey. I feel that the person with whom I am angry deserves at least a day of my silent treatment, or at least ten minutes of my chewing out. So my prayer at this point is: "Make me willing to give up my anger."

A friend of mine, a Christian, gets periodic shock treatments because he is unwilling to let go of anger. Irritations build and continue to build, unresolved until, as his psychiatrist says, "We need to scramble your brains to help you forget the situations that have made you so angry." Obviously, the shock treatments are not solving the problem.

When should we express anger to the person who has triggered the anger within us? The Bible says, "A wise man restrains his anger" (Prov. 19:11, TLB). In other words, "Don't blow up!" Paul wrote "Get over it [your anger] quickly" (Eph. 4:26). "Do we just express anger in prayer? That sounds like we must be a doormat and let people walk all over us. Besides, we can't protect a relationship by holding back our anger. Our dishonesty of restraint could destroy it," we say.

Don't stifle anger. It is going to come out somehow; especially, and particularly, in marriage. Usually we are so close that even though the person is not ventilating anger, we can tell. Actions speak. Vibrations speak. Flying vases speak.

A friend of mine tells of her honeymoon. "Nelson did something that really irritated me. Before I knew it, I had one of our beautiful wedding gifts, a valuable vase in my hand, my arm cocked, ready to fire it at him. I thought of the results: a shattered vase. So, I rolled it at him! We both nearly died laughing."

An open relationship involves communication. Especially in marriage, situations causing anger need to be communicated, but not in an attacking way. Not, "You stinkin' louse! What did you do that for? I hate your guts!" No. Rather, "What you did really made me angry." Communication should continue about the circumstances triggering the anger. Both parties should express their view of the situation, and the problem is worked out, even if it means to agree to disagree. Whether worked out or not, selfish anger is a sin. It needs to be confessed and repented of.

There are times when anger can't be expressed to a spouse. God will be the only recipient of that anger expression (through confession). Possibly the spouse is too threatened to be able to handle it at that time. Or, we're endeavoring to break a pattern of always spewing anger. Consequently, anger is directed to God: "Father, I'm angry." The circumstances can be elaborated. "God, forgive me. Change me. You are my forgiving, loving Savior who can give me a loving spirit for that person."

Then you can go to the partner and say, "You know, I've just gone through a tough time. I've been on my knees and have dealt with my reaction of anger. But your forgetting my birthday today really hurt me. I was very angry about it. I want you to know my feelings, because I know that you want us to have a growing marriage relationship."

Notice the dynamics here. The person has faced, expressed, and resolved the anger within. There was no build-up of destructive physical, psychological, or spiritual symptoms. Communication continued with the partner, building an open and growing relationship. This allows no chance for anyone to become a doormat.

FOUR
The Roots of Anger
*Dealing with
the Source*

We cannot stop here. Thus far we have
dealt with the *sin of anger.* But we must
also deal with the *angry sinner.*

The cure of the sinner is *to die.* The root
cause of most anger is what the Bible calls
sometimes the flesh, the old self, the old
man, the old nature. If we don't get our
way, we get angry. If a perceived need is
not met, we get angry. If our position is
threatened, we get angry. In summary, if
we have an expectation and it isn't met,
the result is anger. We may even say: "I'm
so mad I could die." That is exactly what
we must do. The "I" must die.

"But," you say, "Christ got angry, and
he didn't sin. Besides, if you had to live
with what I have to live with, you would be

angry too. Also, Paul wrote that we should 'be . . . angry, and sin not'" (Eph. 4:26).

Some interpret this Scripture as a command to be angry. But this does not seem to fit the context because five verses later Paul wrote: "Let all bitterness, and wrath, and anger . . . be put away from you" (v. 31). Vine's *Expository Dictionary of New Testament Words* indicates the verse could mean "Be angry of yourselves." I believe it means that even if one is righteously angry (unselfish anger which is not sin), such anger can become sin if one lets it linger without quickly resolving it.

Christians differ over the question of whether all anger is sin. It is my opinion that any result of the flesh, greed, lust, worry, gossip, fear, faithlessness, anger, or impatience is sin, and thus God's potential for us is stifled if we continue in it.

If the root of Christ's anger is examined, we will agree that it was not the result of selfishness. In contrast, as we examine the root of most of our anger, we see that most of it is motivated by selfishness.

A poster of a near-nude girl, boldly displayed outside a Birmingham mall, triggered "righteous anger" in a man passing with his six-year-old son. "Sex is great in marriage," he thought, "but how is my boy going to handle this stimulating picture?" The more he thought about the undue stress this was causing his boy, the angrier he became.

He confronted the store manager. "If you want to sell this seductive material at least keep it inside your shop." He was quickly told to get lost because the poster was a real money-maker.

The father then went to the mall manager and asked if anything could be done about the displayed poster and the problem was taken care of.

Anger in this situation was not sin and it was expressed creatively, with results. But had the man harbored the anger, its poisons would have soon been evident.

Someone has said, "If Eve had gotten angry in the Garden, there would be no sin today." We should get angry at Satan, at sin, at anything anti-Christ.

"Righteous indignation" is a reality, but it is so infrequent that it deserves little ink! Beware! Even if you have diagnosed your anger as righteous, an overindulgence (allowing it to stay overnight) may pass all too easily into sin. James wrote: "For man's anger does not bring about the righteous life that God desires" (James 1:20, NIV).

What does it mean for the "I" to die? The concept of "death of self" is the most dynamic concept I have witnessed in the field of biblical counseling. I will forever be indebted to Charles Solomon for his instruction regarding this concept. For further reading, see his books: *Handbook to Happiness* (Tyndale, 1975); *The Ins and Outs of Rejection* (Notre Dame, IN: Heritage House, 1976); and *Counseling with the Mind of Christ* (Old Tappan, NJ: Revell, 1977).

Paul wrote, "I am crucified with Christ; nevertheless I live; yet not I, but Christ liveth in me" (Gal. 2:20). Paul explained in another place, "Knowing this, that our old man is crucified with him [Christ], that the body of sin might be destroyed, that henceforth we should not serve sin" (Rom. 6:6). May we insert "anger" in place of "sin"? ". . . that the body of [anger] might be destroyed, that henceforth we should not serve [anger]."

If we are Christians, the sin nature within us died with Christ when we received him; consequently, we don't have to be controlled by that old nature any longer.

Its power has been shattered. We find this dynamic described in Romans chapters 6 through 8, Philippians 3, and in Colossians chapters 1 through 3. This is the *insight* perspective of our position in Christ.

This book is not meant to explore too deeply the concepts referred to as identification with Christ, union with Christ, and the deeper walk, terms that describe our position in Christ. There is no point in attempting to duplicate excellent material that is already available which focuses on this distinctive quality of life.

MY TRUE IDENTITY

It is not difficult for most Christians to understand how Christ's death was the sacrifice needed for our sins (justification). As we see how Christ's blood was shed for us to appropriate his forgiveness, we are cleansed and freed from sins.

Too many Christians stop with this insight and are left, as it were, in a spiritual squirrel cage—sinning and confessing, sinning and confessing. Anger explodes or implodes. We confess it. But a short time later the snares of anger thoroughly entrap us again. We confess again. "Is there any freedom from the angry spirit that seems to consume us?" we wonder.

I was not myself

It is usually beneficial for the Christian to find himself in such a position. If there is to be growth in Christ, a person must see his need. Without awareness of need, spiritual growth is minimal.

The Christian is not only to see Christ's death *for* his sins. The Christian must also become aware of the liberating truth of being crucified with Christ *to* his sin nature. Christ, hanging on the cross, bleeding, paid the penalty of our anger. The blood cleanses. But, Christ also took us to the cross with him that we may be delivered from our angry sin nature. "Knowing this, that our old man is crucified with him" (Rom. 6:6). The cross crucifies. The Holy Spirit wants to bring us to freedom from the power of our angry nature.

Since we believe that Christ died for all of us, we should also believe that we have died to the old life we used to live. . . . When someone becomes a Christian he becomes a brand new person inside. He is not the same any more. A new life has begun. . . . For God took the sinless Christ and poured into him our sins. Then in exchange, he poured God's goodness into us! [2 Cor. 5:14, 17, 21, TLB]

Through our crucifixion with him we have died to our self-centered natures. We are completely freed from sin's power whether we take advantage of the freedom or not.

"Hold it, Burwick," you may be thinking. "Are you preaching eradication? I know 'I am crucified with Christ' but the best I can do with my angry nature is try to control it. Do you mean I can actually be freed from it?"

Yes, this is the flawless provision of God's grace. It is not that we cannot sin; but, that we can live without sin. "My little children, I am telling you that so that you will stay away from sin" (1 John 2:1, TLB).

This accomplished fact becomes reality in our experience as moment by moment we count it to be fact. "In the same way, count yourselves dead to sin but alive to God in Christ Jesus" (Rom. 6:11, NIV). Paul elaborated on this further:

Do not let sin control your puny body any longer; do not give in to its sinful desires. Do not let any part of your bodies become tools of wickedness, to be used for sinning; but give yourselves completely to God—every part of you—for you are back from death and you want to be tools in the hands of

God, to be used for his good purposes.
Sin need never again be your master,
for now you are no longer tied to the
law where sin enslaves you, but you are
free under God's favor and mercy.
[Rom. 6:12-14]
We may have felt imprisoned in the
dingiest, darkest, slimiest, hellhole cell of
anger's prison, and have long since given
up making scratch marks on the wall to
record the passing of days and years in
prison.

A way of escape consumes our minds.
We've expressed our anger, which has
seemed to cause only more. We've
"stuffed" our anger and our bodies and
minds have suffered greatly. We've tried to
discuss rationally our anger in the throes of
conflict, but it always seems to boil out of
control. We've gone to the altar; we've
confessed over and over; and we've worn

our plastic smiling Christian faces. But anger is still with us.

Until . . .

The cell door opens. There stands the Master.

"What are you doing in here?" he asks. "Don't you know who you are? Do you want to be released from this prison? You shall know the truth and the truth shall set you free."

"Yes, Master, what is the truth? I want to be free."

"You died with me on the cross when I died. That self-centered nature of yours that gets so angry when it is threatened or doesn't get its way, died with me. Count on that as fact, moment by moment. Yield your whole life to me. Yield those rights and expectations—those desires that push your anger button if they are not fulfilled. As you follow this pattern, the Holy Spirit will make freedom real to you. Through conflicts the truth will become established in you as you yield to the Holy Spirit's power. Be patient. Life-styles don't change overnight. As you see your position in Christ through studying the Word and yielding to it, the Holy Spirit slowly and gently changes life-style. Anger-producing situations are more quickly conquered.

You'll find yourself becoming slower to anger. Let's move on out of this prison cell. You are free."

It is important that we saturate our minds with these Scriptures and allow the Holy Spirit to teach us in depth. Ian Thomas, Watchman Nee, Miles Stanford, Ruth Paxton, and many other authors have excellent material which develops more fully the identification-with-Christ dynamic mentioned here.

As each morning finds us on our knees with Scripture in hand, "renewing our minds" (reminding ourselves that we are not only God's children, but are actually filled through and through with the Creator), our minds are set on our true identity. As we face challenges of the day that could produce anger, we can quickly remind ourselves of who we really are and avoid the poisons of self-centered anger.

For instance, we have the natural expectation of someone close to us meeting specific needs of ours. "I've worked especially hard for this person. I deserve a compliment." The compliment does not come. Our expectation is not met. The natural temptation is to be hurt and angry.

Ideally, as soon as the temptation is

present, we may remind ourselves that we don't have to yield to it. The psalmist wrote: "My soul, wait thou only upon God; for my expectation is from him" (Ps. 62:5). We don't need to expect from anyone, except God, who has promised to supply all our needs (Phil. 4:19). If we really believe these verses and put them into practice, anger and its devastation can be avoided.

However, the ideal is not always achieved. We often hold out for our expectations. When we do, anger can grow and erupt.

When we find ourselves in the throes of anger, any of us can quickly say: "Hold it. I am not acting like who I really am. This angry self died with Christ. I don't have to be controlled by it. And because self is dead, I am alive with the Creator of the universe, who is permeating my very being. He is my strength. He is my life. He is my forgiveness for the unforgivable. He is my love for the unlovely." Thus we are putting into *action* the *insight* we gathered through study and through the teaching of the Holy Spirit.

Jesus said, "Deny [yourself] and take up [your] cross daily" (Luke 9:23). Paul wrote, "Reckon ye also yourselves to be dead indeed unto sin" (Rom. 6:11), meaning by "sin" the old nature. This is the application, the putting into practice or the "shoe leather dynamic" of what we know to be true about ourselves. If we leave out either *insight* or *action,* there will be dysfunction.

Insight-oriented people have a tendency to sit back and expect God to do everything. Action-oriented people take to heart that "non-Scripture," "God helps those who help themselves." Their focus is, "*You* have to die to self," and they tend to lie on their bed of spikes or crawl a mile on their stomachs.

The Bible does say "Mortify [kill] the deeds of the body" (Rom. 8:13). This is important, but it is a lot easier to "die to self" when our minds have been saturated with the concept that we are already dead in Christ, knowing that we just need to yield to that position. The power of our sinful nature is shattered. We don't have to be controlled by it. We just need to act like it, and yield to who we really are.

I am told of an old man who would stand up every Sunday night during the testimony time in church and repeat the same monologue: "Lord, I'm such an evil man. I hate. I lust. I worry. I doubt you. Clean the cobwebs out of my heart." It was the same witness every week—"Clean the cobwebs out of my heart."

It is reported that the last time the old man spoke his piece, he was quickly followed by a little old lady from across the church who stood and said, "Lord, kill the spider."

Confession of sin cleans out the "cobwebs," but *death of self* kills the "spider."

Out of our identification with Christ in death comes our identification with Christ in resurrection. Paraphrasing Paul's words: "It is not I who lives, but Christ through me!"

Consider how this principle might be worked out in an actual life situation: "God, I'm angry at my husband. What he did to me was wrong, and he is responsible for it. But I am responsible for my reaction of anger. I confess it. Take it, God. Change me. I yield to my position of death—death to the right to have a loving husband who will put me first. Lord, you are my security. You are my love. You are my strength. Forgive my husband through me, Lord. Love him through me." Then, we should look for ways to allow God to express that forgiving, loving spirit through us to someone who has made us angry.

Several years ago, my wife and I were near divorce. Our marriage was a hellish mess. We were both working through some scars in our backgrounds, and we were really laying a lot of emotional garbage on each other. Through this trauma, plus severe pregnancy problems for Ann, and then the death of one of our twin boys, we were brought to the end of ourselves.

I am convinced that God must cause or allow such circumstances as this to happen to some Christians so that they can see the utter futility of living in the power of "self." He must bring them to the experience Paul talked about: ". . . in me (that in is my flesh) dwelleth no good thing" (Rom. 7:18).

Only then are we ready for living by the power of the Holy Spirit as described in Romans 8. Only then do we relate to Paul's words: ". . . not because we think we can do anything of lasting value by ourselves. Our only power and success comes from God" (2 Cor. 3:5, TLB).

As this concept became the focus of my wife and me (instead of our pointing a finger at each other), God began to do some drastic work within us. We began to pray, "Jesus, our bitter natures died with you on that cross. We don't have to be controlled by bitterness. We reckon (count on) our old self-life to be dead." As we prayed like that, the bitterness toward each other began to disappear.

FROM DEATH TO LIFE

But there was still a void. Positional death with Christ was becoming an experiential reality. Bitterness was gone. The only feeling was emptiness. Resurrection with Christ had not come into play. I remember very distinctly praying for thirty days straight, "God, I can't love my wife the way you command me to love her. I want to. You love her through me!"

I looked for ways to allow God to express his love through me, even once buying her a rose, although I did not feel like it. On the thirtieth day of the prayer commitment, I noticed a little spark, as the feeling of love began to return. Our love for each other began to return. And our love for each other has continued to deepen and grow since then.

"I am crucified," Paul said. The power of our angry nature is shattered. We need be controlled by it no longer. It is not we who live, but Christ through us.

The mechanics of this concept, called "identification," are much easier to put into "shoe leather" as greater insights are gained.

Some of my clients, while studying identification Scriptures and related material have a very emotional experience. "Wow! Yes, I see! My old self-life died with Christ, and he now lives in and through me!" Burdens are lifted, bondage is broken, and the heavens open!

For some, growth comes through "little glimpses" of identification truth spread over months and years. Our loving heavenly Father gives to his children what we need at the right time, and only as we need it.

PAST ANGER

"The psychiatrist told me I was schizophrenic. Do you think I am, Dr. Burwick?" As he sat in my counseling office, his dark brown eyes sparkled under his teenage crop of stringy hair.

"Let's find out," I replied. Most people I work with who have been labeled "schizo," are bitter people who don't like to face responsibility. "At whom are you angry?"

"I'm not angry," he said. But as we began to talk, severe hatred began to surface. Circumstances from many years past were recalled with such vivid bitterness that Mike would clench his fist and say, "If I could see that guy, I'd kill him!"

Up to this point we have talked about facing and resolving present anger. However, it is also important to resolve the reservoir of past anger that we carry. This angry spirit is usually labeled resentment, bitterness, or hate, and it is the underlying cause of most of the symptoms I see in the counseling office.

Consequently, therapy usually begins with the patient facing the hurts and wrongs that have triggered the resentments. The next step is to exchange these attitudes and feelings for forgiveness. It is amazing how many physical, emotional, mental, spiritual, and social symptoms disappear, sometimes quickly, as forgiveness replaces past resentment.

Paul Tournier, in his book *Violence Within,* states:

Forgiveness is the solution par excellence to every conflict and all violence. But true forgiveness is very rare. Christians try to forgive, because the church tells them they must. But trying to lift oneself up by one's own bootstraps; it is completely ineffective. Because it leaves out of account the grace of God. At best one manages to pretend one has forgiven and that only adds hypocrisy to hostility. The person whom we have wronged is never taken in by the smiling facade. Repressed bitterness of this kind poisons parish life. It is better to tell the truth to each other, even violently. The pretense of forgiveness is an obstacle to forgiveness, just as the pretense of love is an obstacle to love.

In counseling we speak much of hurts. How have you been hurt? What is your deepest hurt? These questions are not designed to cause one to blame others, but to report hurtful situations and identify the natural response to the hurt, which is anger. For if it is unresolved, it leads to the poisonous results of resentment.

FIVE
How to Know You Have Forgiven

The question often arises, "How do I
know if I am really forgiving a person?"
Obviously, the symptoms already
discussed are usually signals of an
unforgiving spirit. But more specifically,
we might ask these questions of ourselves:

1. Do I find myself dwelling on the
offense? Does that hurtful situation often
come back to mind?

2. What kind of feelings do I have
toward that person who hurt (wronged)
me? Do negative feelings persist? Is there
a coolness or resistance on my part? Are
there no feelings of love toward one I am
really supposed to love?

3. Do I find myself rationalizing for that
person? Perhaps we are thinking, "He

didn't mean it." "His parents were that way." She didn't know any better." "Maybe I caused it." This type of understanding is fine if it is preceded by forgiveness. If not, it might indicate that we have only placed a mask over bitterness.

4. Does this bitterness spill over to insignificant situations? Often unresolved anger towards one person diffuses and spills over to others who are not really part of the problem. For example an inordinate amount of anger to policemen, the system, or toward some ethnic group, may be an indication.

Scripture gives us examples of the unforgiving spirit. Worship ought to be a very meaningful experience, but sometimes is not. "Therefore, if you are offering your gift at the altar, and there remember that your brother has something against you, leave your gift there in front of the altar. First, go and be reconciled to your brother; then come and offer your gift." (Matt. 5:23, NIV). We might as well forget about church if we haven't tried to resolve a conflict between us and another person. The ride to church is a favorite time for family conflicts to surface. Shouldn't we apologize before we enter church?

God doesn't forgive me if I am not forgiving another person. Jesus taught us to pray, "Forgive us our debts, as we also have forgiven our debtors . . . . For if you forgive men when they sin against you, your heavenly Father will also forgive you" (Matt. 6:12, NIV). There are different interpretations of this passage, but I believe Jesus was saying that unless we are forgiving one another, we won't sense God's forgiveness of us.

In nearly every severe case of a person who lacks assurance of salvation with whom I have counseled, the underlying cause has been an angry, resentful spirit. As these people worked through their bitterness, applying forgiveness, lack of assurance was no longer a problem.

Unanswered prayer, Jesus taught, is a result of an unforgiving attitude. "Listen to me! You can pray for anything, and if you believe, you have it; it's yours! But when you are praying, first forgive anyone you are holding a grudge against, so that your Father in heaven will forgive your sins too" (Mark 11:24, 25, TLB).

Mind in turmoil, as I describe a certain behavior pattern, is caused by an unforgiving spirit. "And his lord was wroth, and delivered him to the tormentors, till he should pay all that was due unto him. So likewise shall my heavenly Father do also unto you, if ye from your hearts forgive not every one his brother their trespasses" (Matt. 18:34, 35). Most mental torment is a result of an unforgiving spirit, or pent-up anger.

MIND IN TURMOIL

My beautiful wife, through whom the Lord has so richly blessed and continues to bless me, had a classic experience of *mind in turmoil.*

Some years ago, although walking in fellowship with the Lord, she began to have weird thinking patterns, such as false guilt and irrational fears—fear of losing control, of insanity, fear of being alone. She didn't want me to go to work. She had a guilt-induced compulsion to confess for anything. If she stepped on an ant, she had to confess that as sin, if she used a metal spatula on someone's Teflon pan, that was a tormenting sin that had to be confessed over and over.

She went through hours of deep introspection, trying to sort out these fears, the reality of them, and their possible cause. At times she felt as if she were outside her body seeing herself and others from a distance, looking from the outside into a discussion.

She seemed to be losing her mind, and I feared for her life. In fact, she often said, "Ray, just commit me to the mental institution so I won't hurt anyone."

As desperation and despair increased, God used Dr. Henry Brandt, a Christian psychologist and author of many books, to show us God's answer. Dr. Brandt unselfishly and graciously agreed to meet us at the Seattle, Washington, airport. Dr. Brandt arrived from the north; we from the east, and the three-hour encounter began.

Before long, Dr. Brandt was lovingly, gently, yet firmly saying, "Ann, you have much bitterness within you." She denied it. How could such a loving, super-sweet person be filled with bitterness?

Before the session ended, Ann began to catch a glimpse of the pent-up anger within. Dr. Brandt told her to confess it whether or not it was apparent and to ask God to cleanse her angry spirit.

We left the airport excited that there was an answer and very grateful to Dr. Brandt. But we in no way realized that the next three years would be marked by trauma and pain, resulting in a tremendously purifying experience that would see God remaking both Ann and me.

Jeremiah wrote "I did as he told me, and found the potter working at his wheel. But the jar that he was forming didn't turn out as he wished, so he kneaded it into a lump and started again. Then the Lord said: O Israel [Ray and Ann], can't I do to you as this potter has done to this clay? As the clay is in the potter's hand, so are you in my hand" (Jer. 18:3-6, TLB).

Ann's symptoms of weird thinking began to disappear rapidly. She studied positive Scripture daily. Introspection was curtailed. She gave more of herself to others. When a weird thought or fear would come to mind she would pray, "Lord, I know what I am thinking is not true, although it certainly seems to be. I know this is a coverup for pent-up anger. I don't even feel my anger now, God, but I confess it to you as the cause of this symptom. God, take my angry spirit. Love and forgive through me."

Within two weeks, most of the symptoms were gone. However, the deep anger that had been lying dormant for years began to surface. Because of my insecurity, I began to be very reactive, threatened, and angry. Much of my inner ugliness surfaced. Oh, the pain and trauma that ensued within and between both of us!

C. S. Lewis said, "God whispers to us in our pleasures. He speaks to us through our conscience, and shouts at us in our pain. Pain is God's megaphone to arouse a deaf world." God was shouting at us, getting us ready for our next encounter with a godly man who would share more truth with us.

Two and a half years after God blessed us with Dr. Brandt's visit, he led us to Dr. Charles Solomon. Through his teaching we began to learn the dynamic concept of seeing our sin nature, the cause of our anger and self-centeredness, as dead in Christ; and because of that, we now live with the power of the Creator alive in us. What a growing, enlightening time it has been since!

Ann's "mind in turmoil" was caused by pent-up anger, an unforgiving spirit. As she learned to face her anger, confess and repent of it, and as she learned to forgive me and others who had wronged her, her mind became one of peace and strength.

Paul wrote, "For God hath not given us the spirit of fear; but of power, and of love, and of a sound mind" (2 Tim. 1:7). Most of her symptoms left quickly, but a life-style is not changed overnight.

As she has allowed God to cleanse her of her sin of anger, to show her her co-death with his Son, to reveal her new life lived by the power of the Holy Spirit, making her able to forgive the unforgivable, she is becoming a radiant, beautiful, outstanding woman.

SIX
The How-to of Forgiveness

At this point, someone may be asking,
"How does a person forgive another who
has really wronged him?" First we should
define the word.

There are many definitions for the word
"forgive." I like my wife's best: "Bear
the reality of the hurt; then, choose to
remember it against him (or her) no
longer." The person who forgives faces
completely the extent of hurt or wrong
dealt to him. He doesn't rationalize for it
or for the person who offended him. He
doesn't block it out of his mind. He doesn't
cover or mask it with alcohol, drugs, shock
treatments, or a life-style of busy-ness. He
sets the offender free from the wrong and
wipes the slate clean.

"Just a minute. There is no way I can forgive my stepfather," said a young woman sitting in my office. "I wish God would burn him in hell, and before he does, I hope he will do everything to him that he did to me. I can't pick up a coat hanger without remembering the times he beat me with hangers. I can't touch water to my face without remembering the times he held my head under water until I would submit to his cruel sexual advances.

"Forgive him? You're kidding! I want him to be displayed in pornography like he did me. I want him to experience the sexual brutality he gave me that even now prohibits me from bearing children.

"I want his teeth broken off at the roots by a phone being smashed into his face like he did to me . . . tied to a bed with scalding water thrown on him . . . taken to the woods to stand naked for hours . . . burnt with cigarettes . . . pushed down the stairs . . . kept prisoner in his own house for ten years without a friend . . . [and more that is too cruel and lewd to mention here] . . . like he did me! How can I but hate him?

"I want him to experience what I am going through now: the overwhelming fears, depression, panic attacks, loss of

memory, nightmares. I want a psychiatrist
to tell him he'll have to spend weeks in
a mental hospital. And you say I have to
forgive him? He deserves more than the
seven years in prison he got! He deserves
hell!"

Suppose you are the counselor. What
would your reactions be? Part of me
wanted to weep for the hurt Gail (not her
real name) has experienced. Part of me
wanted to strangle that "animal"
stepfather. Yet, God says, "Vengeance
is mine. I will repay."

STEPS OF FORGIVENESS

The following were the steps I gently
persuaded Gail to walk through to help her
get over the anger that was controlling her.

1. "Gail, you are over the first hurdle,"
I told her. "The Bible indicates that we are
to let God search our hearts for any
destructive attitude or acts (Ps. 139:23,
24). You are facing squarely your
stepfather's wrong and your reaction of
hate and bitterness. Now, so that you no
longer remain tied to him and continue to
reap his cruelty, we must begin the
forgiveness process." (I said "we" because
I felt she needed direction and God's
power to accomplish the task.)

2. The next step was to apply Philippians 2:13: "For God is at work within you, helping you want to obey him, and then helping you do what he wants" (TLB). She needed to learn to pray, "Lord, my desire is to see that man burn in hell. Give me the desire to let go of my hatred so that I can forgive him."

This could become a "cop-out" prayer. At times I see persons entrenched in this prayer for weeks. Their attitudes don't match their words. There is no way they want to resolve the problem, so they lay the blame on God for not making them willing.

3. Gail needed to learn to pray, "Yes, Lord, I will forgive. Work a consistent spirit of forgiveness through me to him. Father, as you forgave me when I did not deserve to be forgiven, so I forgive my stepfather whether he deserves it or not."

Any Carmichael stated it, "If I feel bitter toward those who condemn me unjustly (or so it seems to me), then I am forgetting that if they knew me as I know myself, they would condemn me much more." Though the process of forgiveness begins with an initial act of the will, it must be remembered that deep forgiveness of a deep hurt sometimes takes a considerable time.

4. As Step 3 was operating, two other aspects of forgiveness needed to take place. Gail needed to pray, "God, forgive me! My hate, my resentment is sin. Cleanse me."

The Lord's Prayer petitions God to forgive us as we have forgiven others. Before we can ask for our sins to be forgiven we should be in the process of forgiving others who have sinned against us.

We should realize that these important truths about forgiveness are really applicable only to Christians. A non-Christian must first establish a sonship with God before he claims the rights of sonship. "To all who received him [Christ], to those who believed in his name, he gave the right to become children of God" (John 1:12, NIV). If a person is not sure he or she is a child of God, it should be known that an explanation of how to become a member of God's family is given in the appendix of this book.

If a person does not desire to become a member of God's family, the best anyone could do for him is to encourage him to face his anger; express it creatively so as not to attack others; endeavor to become more selfless, so that when he doesn't get his way there will be less chance for anger; and to find a physical outlet for tension produced by anger, such as jogging, swimming, or hard physical work.

In the forgiveness dynamic, it is sometimes necessary to forgive oneself. At times it is difficult to forgive ourselves, but it is an essential ingredient in the forgiveness process for some situations. If your anger has been vented in a malicious, slandering way, it could cause severe guilt, which needs forgiveness of self. One should not block it out, trying to forget it. The shadow world of the past will haunt us until we can face the mirror and say, "What I did was wrong. I have been forgiven of God. I now forgive myself."

For Gail, forgiving herself was not a significant issue.

5. When there is a conflict between two people, a solution is to contact the other person involved and seek forgiveness for our part of the conflict. Some people appear to carry this too far and cause tremendous turmoil. Only if there is

obvious conflict between the two should this step be taken.

"What if the person doesn't forgive me? Then what do I do?" someone may ask. Their reaction is their responsibility. If they don't forgive us, that is their problem. We have done our part. We must, however, maintain a forgiving, caring attitude toward the other person and allow God to finish the work.

6. If the hurtful memory, that which has been forgiven, returns, it usually means one of three things is happening:

a. We gave mental assent to forgive, but didn't mean it.

b. Satan is attacking. Ephesians 4:26, 27 indicates that Satan gets a mighty foothold through our resentments. He must be rebuked and told to leave us alone (1 Pet. 5:9).

c. The forgiveness for that situation was not a climactic event, but the beginning of a process. We must keep the process going by saying: "Yes, I am choosing to remember that sin against that person no longer."

Whatever the case, we must not dwell on the memory. We must rebuke Satan, tell him to flee (James 4:7), and remind ourselves that according to Romans 6:6, our old sinful nature died with Christ. We need not be controlled by an unforgiving spirit. Christ lives in us, willing to produce forgiveness and love through us to that person.

"I may not forget, but I am *willing* to forget" is far better than the fallacious statement, "I can forgive, but I can't forget!" The latter is a signal that we really don't want to forgive.

As forgiveness begins to take place, a grateful attitude develops toward the offender. We begin to see how God is using the hurtful situation and the offender's wrong (sin) to develop strength of character in us. We are actually better people because of the trauma.

This is depicted in Scripture by Joseph in Genesis 37—50. Joseph was rejected by his brothers, sold into slavery, blackmailed, and imprisoned. Then he had the chance to get even with his brothers who had caused his pain. Joseph's reaction? "What you meant for evil," he said, "God planned for good." He saw how his brothers' evil resulted in his own strength and success. Joseph forgave!

THANKS FOR STUTTERING

All parents make mistakes. I was once very resentful toward mine for mistakes they made in child rearing that helped to formulate a grotesque stuttering speech pattern in me.

I had terrible fears of speaking. I often got humg up on a word and could not say it, sometimes even dislocating my jaw trying to say a word. A taped basketball TV show had to be cancelled because my stuttering ruined the presentation (days before Mel Tillis!). Tears of embarrassment and anger often streaked my cheeks.

But now I would not change it for the world, even if I could do it all over again and be free of stuttering. Because of stuttering, I became a good listener. I couldn't talk, what choice did I have but to listen? I have developed a very empathetic spirit in relating to hurting people because I have been there. Stuttering has driven me to a deep relationship with God. Where I am weak, he has become strong (2 Cor. 12:10). I believe I am an effective counselor mainly because of these dynamics. Now I can say, "Thank you, God, for my stuttering. Thank you, Dad and Mom, for your strengths and your weaknesses!" I wasted a lot of energy and suffered much discomfort because of all that resentment that I carried for years.

Is your life full of difficulties and temptations? Then be happy, for when the way is rough, your patience has a chance to grow. So let it grow, and don't try to squirm out of your problems. For when your patience is finally in full bloom, then you will be ready for anything, strong in character, full and complete. [James 1:2-4, TLB]

Praise the Lord! As you and I forgive others for pain they have caused us, the spirit of God builds in us strong character until we are "full and complete." Our gratitude turns to praise, and praise is the greatest decentralizer of self that there is. Getting eyes off of self and circumstances and onto God and others alleviates much personal discomfort!

The process of forgiveness is terminated as we can pray that God would richly bless the offender, and as we express love by giving of our time, talent, our means to that person, not expecting anything in return.

SEVEN
The Results of Forgiveness

I wish I could say that all of my clients leave the counseling office free from paranoia, physical symptoms, weird thinking, anxiety, marital hangups, and depression. There are some who obviously want to continue hanging onto and hugging the hurts, drinking the poison of bitterness at their solitary pity-party. Others I may have turned off by a tendency I have to try to rush in and fix it, causing the counseling process to abort.

But words cannot express the joy and fulfillment I feel when I walk through the fiery furnace of hurts and hates with a client and see them allow God to bring them out unburned. In fact, they appear from the furnace stronger people, with the only indication of burning being the absence of fetters of fears, insecurities, resentments, and guilts. Only these fetters that bound them were burned.

I must finish the story of Gail. Her symptoms grew worse. She became a prisoner in her own home, except when she went out for a quick jog, which was part of my prescription for depression. On a fateful Tuesday, she became so disoriented while jogging that she lost her way. She had to stop a passerby to ask where she lived. To her chagrin, the person pointed her to her house just three houses away.

She called me in a tremendous depression. My words to her were that the distortion of memory, the depression, the weird thinking were mostly tied to her hate for her stepfather. "Gail, even if you need to go to a church group and request support prayer, do it. You must let go of all of that hate. Possibly a group praying for you would help you let go of it and replace it with a forgiving, loving attitude." That was around one o'clock in the afternoon.

At about five o'clock I received a call from Gail saying, "Ray, I'm free!" In Gail's words, "Something just had to happen. I said to myself, I am a Christian, and I shouldn't have to be going through this. If this is related to my hate for my stepfather, I had better resolve it. So I called my stepfather in Australia. After some difficulty, we located him. I was scared to death. What would I hear on the other end of the line? Would I receive a blast of dirty profanity? I said 'Hello, Jim, this is Gail!'

"He very nearly came through the phone. 'Oh, Gail. It's so good to hear you. I've spent thousands of dollars on private investigators, trying to locate you. I've been saved, and I do so much need you to forgive me for the terrible way I treated you. I'll do anything. My weekly paycheck is yours for the rest of my life if that would bring about your forgiveness.'

"Ray, he was in tears," she said, "As we talked, it seemed as if a dark, oppressing cloud lifted from me. We hung up, and immediately I saw a coat hanger in my room. Ray, I could pick up that hanger without the terrible memories reappearing of the scores of times he had beaten me with a coat hanger. And, Ray, tonight I'm going to take my first bath in seventeen years." She had showered, but hadn't been able to bathe because of the memories of being held under water until she would yield to his cruel, selfish demands.

The next morning Gail called to say, "Ray, I took my first bath in seventeen years. I went to the shopping center and could ride an escalator without holding on for dear life. My loss of memory is minimal. I'm free!"

It would be nice if every story ended like this. Unfortunately, when people give themselves to a spirit of resentment, anger, or hatred, unknowingly they give Satan a mighty foothold. "If you are angry, don't sin by nursing your grudge. Don't let the sun go down with you still angry—get over it quickly; for when you are angry, you give a mighty foothold to the devil" (Eph. 4:26, 27, TLB).

Of late, I have been made aware of a frightening dynamic. Combine what we just saw in Ephesians 4:26, 27 with Ephesians 6:10-12 (TLB):

Last of all I want to remind you that your strength must come from the Lord's mighty power within you. Put on all of God's armor so that you will be able to stand safe against all strategies and tricks of Satan. For we are not fighting against people made of flesh and blood, but against persons without bodies—the evil rulers of the unseen world, those mighty satanic beings and great evil princes of darkness who rule this world; and against huge numbers of wicked spirits in the spirit world.

Recently, one of my clients was made aware of the fact that she was fighting forces of the unseen world. As a Christian, she had unknowingly allowed a volcano of bitterness to build up in her. A psychiatrist had made a zombie of her for six years on a hundred-dollar-a-month drug treatment. She finally saw the futility and came off all drugs "cold turkey." She saw a pastoral counselor who helped her immensely. She counseled with me nine times over a six-month period, and she saw great relief from most of her depression, anxiety, and disoriented thinking. She had many months of peace, joy, and rejuvenated life-style.

Then some weird symptoms reappeared. At that time, an evangelist was speaking at her church. He was experienced in dealing with satanic activity, but he was not a wild-eyed exorcist. They met upon the advice of her physician. After a few minutes, it was apparent that she was under demonic power. After forty-five minutes of discussion and prayer, she was released from oppression.

"Incredible!" you may say. I don't understand it, and up to this point, I have had very little experience with this phenomenon. Did Satan's power gain a measure of control over her when she was drugged for so long? Did her repressed anger give Satan a foothold? I don't know! It bears our concern, because Scripture speaks of it.

Getting back to Gail: She was so overwhelmed by the hatred toward her stepfather that she was unaware of the subtle resentments building within her towards her neighbors, her work, her husband, and various other targets. It took her some time even to admit to and then to face the large reservoir of anger within.

The following weeks were tumultuous. Along with the tremendous reservoir of anger, she became aware of her need to control and dominate those around her. She saw her great need for attention as she would pour out her trouble to anyone who would listen. She rebelled against her husband's leadership. She saw her wanton waste of money. It was difficult to face. There were days when she would plead for escape—to Australia, to the hospital. There were times when she would blame everyone else, and her mind would again become disoriented. There were days she would call "the greatest I have lived. I see all my hate, my irresponsibility and my rebellion. I am letting the Lord have them. He is changing me." As these better days became more frequent, her symptoms dissipated, antidepressants and tranquilizers were phased out, and she became a vibrant testimony for Jesus Christ.

The lesson we learn here is that for personal growth, a consistency must be maintained—consistency in (1) *awareness:* not allowing anger to build up; daily study of Scripture to know God and self better; (2) *Action:* irresponsibility faced and resolved; yielding to who we really are in Christ.

GROUCHINESS MAY BE A GOOD SIGN
Sudden irritability, quarrelsomeness, and complaining in a person who for years has suffered depression are to be looked on as signs of improvement. Chicago psychiatrist Samuel H. Kraines, M.D., offers the example of a woman who was soft-spoken and gentle before her depression. As she

starts to recover from her "illness," she may become a "screaming shrew, pouring forth a torrent of abuse."

This period of excessive irritability may last anywhere from one to three months and disappear as suddenly as it erupted. Although the condition may be hard to cope with, Dr. Kraines sees this period as part of "an ascending curve," approaching recovery. Other signs of patient improvement are weight gain, intense fatigue, and memory loss. Dr. Kraines emphasizes that these symptoms indicate impending recovery; they are not assurances that the patient has been cured of his disease. "It's like seeing the first robin," said Dr. Kraines. "There is still some cold weather left."

FUTURE ANGER

Past anger (resentment, bitterness, hate) is resolved by confession, repentance, cleansing, forgiveness, and yielding. Present anger is resolved through expression and turning from it. But what about future anger? "I don't want to be such an angry person. How can I become free of it, and what can I do to solve this anger problem?" someone may ask.

I may be accused of oversimplification at

this point, but the answer is simply *yield.* Yield to who we *really* are. We can say, "I'm a child of God. He loves me and wants to bless me richly. He promises that all things work together for my good, conforming me to the image of Christ. Thus, the irritation I'm experiencing now can produce not anger but (1) tolerance, after which I'll have even stronger character; or (2) sensitivity to the needs of others."

For example, my family lives with a father and husband who is still too rigid. When Ann calls for dinner and I leave my very significant activity, I expect the food to be on the table ready to serve. Quite often it's still in the process. "Now who does she think she is—keeping his eminence waiting?" And when I'm in my rigid mood, I sure let her know of the terrible inconvenience she has caused me! How would you like to live with someone like that?

Ann has a choice of response to my rigidity—anger, or love and acceptance. Her prayer at that moment can be "God, change that turkey so he'll be more pleasant to live with," or, "Lord, you are the grace I need now to forgive Ray, to love him, and accept him as he is. Work through me the gentleness I need now to confront him lovingly with the rigidity which makes him unhappy."

Ann and I have covenanted that we will not ask God to change the other until he has finished using that particular irritation to "perfect" us. Ann would pray, "Lord, don't change Ray's rigidness until you are finished using it to reshape and build me."

When God's purpose in our life is achieved through an irritation, he is then free to remove that irritation from our life, or keep it for a permanent blessing in our development as a Christian. Paul wrote:

To keep me from becoming conceited because of these surpassingly great revelations, there was given me a thorn in my flesh, a messenger of Satan, to torment me. Three times I pleaded with the Lord to take it away from me. But he said to me, "My grace is sufficient for you, for my power is made perfect in weakness." Therefore, I will boast all the more gladly about my weaknesses, so that Christ's power may rest on me. That is why, for Christ's sake, I delight in weaknesses, in insults, in hardships, in persecutions, in difficulties. For when

I am weak, then I am strong.
[2 Cor. 12:7-10, NIV]

However, if we retreat from irritations,
God must either continually allow for
further irritations or set aside his greatest
plan for our life. Our prayers should be:

"Thank you, Lord, for that alcoholic
husband, that nagging wife, that unfair
boss, my singlehood. I'm your child. I'm
committed to follow you, so I am your
responsibility. You want the best for me;
so thank you for (person's name) and the
ultimate blessing that will result."

Our response of gratitude to God for
every irritation frees us to discover the
ultimate blessing to be gained. If we can't
give thanks, irritations drip their poisons
into our cesspool of anger until the stench
so permeates our being that people flee
from our presence.

A tool that I have found helpful in
creating a "yielded to God" mind-set for
the day is the following early morning
funeral-resurrection ceremony I often have:

Father, I greet you this morning,
realizing if there is sin in my life, you
won't give attention to my prayer
[Ps. 66:18]. By the power of your Holy

Spirit, reveal to me any sin I may be carrying [Ps. 139:23, 24].

Father, am I harboring any resentment? [Mark 11:25]. Reveal this to me so I can forgive—that I be forgiven of you.

Do I need to go to someone and rectify a wrong? [Matt. 5:23, 24].

This is the day the Lord has made. We will rejoice and be glad in it [Ps. 118:24, TLB].

No good thing will he withhold from those who walk along his paths [Ps. 84:11, TLB].

For it was I, Jehovah your God, who brought you out of the land of Egypt. Only test me! Open your mouth wide and see if I won't fill it. You will receive every blessing you can use! [Ps. 81:10, TLB].

Let everyone bless God and sing his praises, for he holds our lives in his hands. And he holds our feet to the path. You have purified us with fire, O Lord, like silver in a crucible. You captured us in your net and laid great burdens on our backs. You sent troops to ride across our broken bodies. We went through fire and flood. But in the end, you brought us into wealth and great abundance" [Ps. 66:8-12, TLB].

God is our refuge and strength, a tested help in times of trouble. And so we need not fear even if the world blows up, and the mountains crumble into the sea [Psalm 46:1-2].

I waited patiently for God to help me; then he listened and heard my cry. He lifted me out of the pit of despair, out from the bog and the mire, and set my feet on a hard, firm path and steadied me as I walked along. He has given me a new song to sing, of praises to our God. Now many will hear of the glorious things he did for me, and stand in awe before the Lord, and put their trust in him. Many blessings are given to those who trust the Lord, and have no confidence in those who are proud, or who trust in idols [Ps. 40:1-4].

Be delighted with the Lord. Then he will give you all your heart's desires. Commit everything you do to the Lord. Trust him to help you do it and he will . . . . Rest in the Lord; wait patiently for him to act [Ps. 37:4-7].

Father, I want to remind myself this morning that my sin-loving nature died

with your Son when he died; my pride,
my resentments, my lust, my expectations, my rights, my need for approval,
my preferences, my will were nailed to
the cross with him. I am no longer
under sin's control. Instead, I am alive to
God [Rom. 6:1-13]. The Creator of the
universe is inhabiting my very being.
Live through me today as you choose,
so that I may say as Jesus did, that I do
nothing of myself, but live
by the power of the living Father
[John 5:19; 6:57].

This day is yours. I realize that
anything that comes my way today,
whether promotion or deposing [Ps.
75:6], victory or defeat, blessing or
testing, mountain or valley, has come
with your permission. It has come with
great purpose from my loving heavenly
Father to bless me and conform me to
the image of Jesus Christ [Rom. 8:28,
29]. And since you spared not your
Son, but gave him up for me, won't
you surely give me everything else?
[Rom. 8:32].

Today, I am more than conqueror
through Christ [Rom. 8:37] to live,
to love, and to give [1 Cor. 13].

"Just a minute, Burwick," you say. "That sounds nice, but it sure makes it look as if I have to be a doormat. I have been a doormat too long. What I need now is assertiveness training."

Jesus gave us a great example of attitude and action. His attitude was one of tenderness, kindness, and forgiveness. His action was comparable, yet also very tough at times. He drove the money-changers out of the temple with whips. He lambasted the religious leaders for their hypocrisy. Jesus was tough and tender.

Along with our forgiving spirit, there is a place for a tough "No. What you are doing is wrong. I can't let you continue to do that."

The first time Christ sent his disciples out, he instructed them to go only with the clothes on their backs (Luke 10:4). However, in Luke 22:36, he commands them to take extra provisions—even a sword! "If you have no sword, better sell your clothes and buy one."

There is a place for both passive and assertive trust in God. "God, grant us the wisdom to know when to be tender—when to be tough."

THE CHALLENGE

We should ask ourselves: "Is there any grudge, any resentment I am carrying? God, show me a face or a name or someone about whom I am carrying bitterness of which I am not aware."

God may answer this prayer instantaneously, or he may cause circumstances to develop in the next few days that will let us know if there is someone we need to forgive. We shouldn't be surprised if we remember something that goes back into childhood. There may still be resentment toward our parents, or brothers, or sisters. There may still be hurts from our dating days. We shouldn't be too quick to say, "No, there is nothing." We need to spend time with the Lord on this question, allowing the Holy Spirit to search our souls.

When the Lord brings something to mind, we should pray: "Lord, forgive me for carrying around these hurtful emotions. Cleanse me from resentment. I need your power and grace to forgive (person's name) for the wrong inflicted on me."

This is not a one-time prayer, but an attitude that must be maintained consistently until the forgiveness process terminates, and the resentment—the ill will—is gone.

We should treat pent-up anger as a poisonous viper, confess it, flee from it, and resolve it as quickly as possible. Then we can be free—free from turbulence, turmoil, and the pain of pent-up anger— free to love and be loved, free on the journey of becoming all that God has created us to become.

APPENDIX 1
Becoming a Member of the Family of God

"For God so loved the world that he gave his only begotten Son, that whosoever believeth in him should not perish, but have everlasting life" (John 3:16). Jesus died for you. Believe in him and receive eternal life.

"Believe on the Lord Jesus Christ, and thou shalt be saved" (Acts 16:31). Believing one has one hundred dollars in the bank does no good until he acts upon the belief.

Jesus said, "I am the way, the truth, and the life; no man cometh unto the Father, but by me" (John 14:6). Jesus is the *only* way.

"But as many as received him, to them gave he the power [the right] to become the sons of God, even to them that believe on his name" (John 1:12). By an act of your will—not feelings—you receive Christ. Ask him to come into your life, and take residence in your life.

"For it is by grace you have been saved, through faith—and this not from yourselves, it is the gift of God—not by works, so that no one can boast" (Eph. 2:8, 9, NIV). Living a good life does not get you to heaven. Receiving God's gift of salvation is your entrance fee.

"Behold, I stand at the door and knock; if any one hears my voice and opens the door, I will come in to him" (Rev. 3:20, RSV). Why not open the door of your life to allow Christ to enter!

Receiving Christ involves turning to God from self, trusting Christ to come into our lives to forgive our sins and to make us what he wants us to be. It is not enough to give intellectual assent to his claims or to have an emotional experience. We must, by an act of our will, ask Jesus Christ to come into our lives, forgive us, and turn us around from a self-centered life to a God- and others-centered life.

If you have not made the discovery of knowing Christ personally, may I invite you to receive Christ as your Savior and Lord now? Your attitude, not words, is what is important; but it may be very helpful to pray this prayer:

Lord Jesus, thank you for loving me and dying for my sins. I need you. I now receive you as my Savior and Lord. I turn from my old life and expect a new life in you. Thank you for forgiving my sins and giving me life forever with you.

Saying these words did not give you the gift of salvation. But if your attitude is depicted by these words, then Christ is in you and wants to give you an abundant life.

Learn about this truth of salvation. Get to know God better. Time with God each day in studying, praying, and meditating is very important. Most Christian bookstores have literature pertaining to Christian growth. The Gospel of John in the New Testament is an excellent place to begin study. Attendance at a Bible-believing church is important.

Knowing God better helps us know ourselves better and, in turn, helps us to see the resources we have in him to change those areas of our lives that need changing.

APPENDIX 2
Anger and Bitterness in the Bible

BITTER

Psalm 64:2, 3	"Hide me from the secret counsel of the wicked; from the insurrection of the workers of iniquity: who whet their tongue like a sword and bend their bows to shoot their arrows, even bitter words."
Proverbs 5:3, 4	"For the lips of a strange woman drop as an honeycomb, and her mouth is smoother than oil: But her end is bitter

as wormwood, sharp as a two-edged sword."

Ecclesiastes 7:26 "And I find more bitter than death the woman whose heart is snares and nets, and her hands as bands: whoso pleaseth God shall escape from her; but the sinner shall be taken by her."

Colossians 3:19 "Husbands, love your wives and be not bitter against them."

James 3:10, 11 "Out of the same mouth proceedeth blessing and cursing. My brethren, these things ought not to be so. Doth a fountain send forth at the same place sweet water and bitter?"

James 3:13, 14 "If you are wise, live a life of steady goodness, so that only good deeds will pour forth. And if you don't brag about them, then you will be truly wise! And by all means don't brag about being wise and good if you are bitter and jealous and selfish; that is the worst sort of lie" (TLB).

BITTERNESS

Job 21: 23, 25   "One dieth in his full strength, being wholly at ease and quiet . . . . and another dieth in the bitterness of his soul, and never eateth with pleasure."

Proverbs 14:10   "Only the person involved can know his own bitterness or joy— no one else can really share it" (TLB).

Acts 8:23   "For I perceive that thou art in the gall of bitterness, and in the bond of iniquity."

Hebrews 12:15   "Look after each other so that not one of you will fail to find God's

best blessings. Watch
out that no bitterness
takes root among you,
for as it springs up it
causes deep trouble,
hurting many in their
spiritual lives" (TLB).

ANGER

Psalm 37:8 "Cease from anger, and
forsake wrath; fret not
thyself in any wise to do
evil."

Proverbs 15:1 "A soft answer turns
away wrath, but harsh
words cause quarrels"
(TLB).

Proverbs 15:18 "A quick-tempered man
starts fights; a cool-
tempered man tries to
stop them" (TLB).

Proverbs 16:32 "It is better to be slow-
tempered than famous;
it is better to have self-
control than to control
an army" (TLB).

Proverbs 19:11 "A wise man restrains
his anger and overlooks

insults. This is to his credit" (TLB).

Proverbs 20:2   "The king's fury is like that of a roaring lion; to rouse his anger is to risk your life" (TLB).

Proverbs 21:14   "An angry man is silenced by giving him a gift" (TLB).

Proverbs 22:8   "He that soweth iniquity shall reap vanity; and the rod of his anger shall fail."

Proverbs 27:4   "Jealousy is more dangerous and cruel than anger" (TLB).

Ecclesiastes 7:9   "Be not hasty in thy spirit to be angry; for anger resteth in the bosom of fools."

Matthew 5:22   "But I say to you that every one who is angry with his brother shall be liable to judgment; whoever insults his brother shall be liable to the council, and whoever says, 'you fool!' shall be liable to the hell of fire" (RSV).

Ephesians 4:31	"Stop being mean, bad-tempered and angry. Quarreling, harsh words, and dislike of others should have no place in your lives" (TLB).
Colossians 3:8	"But now is the time to cast off and throw away all these rotten garments of anger, hatred, cursing, and dirty language" (TLB).
Colossians 3:21	"Fathers, provoke not your children to anger, lest they be discouraged."
Colossians 3:21	"Fathers, don't scold your children so much that they become discouraged and quit trying" (TLB).
1 Timothy 2:8	"I will therefore that men pray every where,

lifting up holy hands, without wrath and doubting."

2 Timothy 2:16   "Steer clear of foolish discussions which lead people into the sin of anger with each other" (TLB).

James 1:19, 20   "Let every man be quick to hear, slow to speak, slow to anger, for the anger of men does not work the righteousness of God" (RSV).

EXAMPLES OF ANGER
Cain *(Gen. 4:3-8)*
1. God rejected his offering.
2. Anger; depression; face dark with fury; murder.

Esau *(Gen. 27:41)*
1. Hated Jacob for his deceit.
2. Plotted murder.
3. Tears of bitterness (27:34).

Joseph's brothers *(Gen. 37:4-20)*
1. Jealousy.
2. Hate.
3. Death plotted; revenge.

Saul *(1 Sam. 18:8—31:4)*
1. Rejection: people praised David and not Saul.
2. Jealousy (v. 9).
3. Raved like a madman.
4. Murder attempt on David.
5. Fear-hatred syndrome (v. 29).
6. Murder attempt on his own son (20:33).
7. Paranoia (22:7-9).
8. Murdered priests (22:18).
9. Spiritism; mediums consulted.
10. Suicide (31:4).

Ahab *(1 Kings 22:8-27)*
1. Micaiah didn't meet his expectations in that he wouldn't prophesy good for him.
2. Hate; revenge.

Naaman *(2 Kings 5:9-15)*
1. Elisha instructs him to wash in the Jordan for his leprosy.

2. Pride.

3. Anger; rage.

4. Repentance; healed; humble.

King Asa *(2 Chron. 16:7-13)*

1. Placed trust in man instead of God.

2. Rebuked by prophet.

3. Anger; jailed prophet.

4. Foot disease; sought cure through men, not God.

5. Died two years later.

Haman *(Esther 3:5—7:10)*

1. Pride.

2. Hate; revenge.

3. Plotted murder of Jews.

4. Hanged on his own gallows.

Nebuchadnezzar *(Dan. 3:13, 19-26)*

1. Pride.

2. So full of fury his face changed.

3. "Murder" of mighty soldiers.

4. Attempted murder of three others.

Herodias *(Mark 6:18-28)*

1. John confronted Herod about the king's sexual sin.

2. Herodias angry; revenge.
3. John beheaded.

Enemies of Christ *(Luke 6:11)*
   1. Wild with rage.
   2. Plotted his murder.

RESULTS OF RESENTMENT

Genesis 27:45	Separates brothers
Genesis 30:2	Separates husband and wife
Genesis 49:6	Leads to murder
Numbers 11:1	Brings judgment from God
Psalm 64:2, 3	Causes devious plotting and accusations
Proverbs 14:17	Causes foolish behavior and hatred of others
Proverbs 20:2	Retaliation and judgment
Proverbs 21:19	Causes others to avoid us
Proverbs 22:24, 25	Causes others to become like us
Proverbs 29:22	Causes strife and sin

Isaiah 38:15, 17	Loss of sleep; depression
Jonah 4:9	Temptation to suicide
Matthew 5:22	Brings judgment
Matthew 18:34, 35	Torment
Acts 8:23	Envy which leads to sin
Colossians 3:21	Discourages children
Titus 3:3	Brings division, hatred of others
Hebrews 12:15	Defiles others
James 3:14-16	Brings confusion, evil work
1 John 2:8-11	Leads to darkness and confusion

EXAMPLES OF FORGIVENESS

| Genesis 50:20 | Joseph after brothers sold him to slavery: "Ye thought evil against me: but God meant it unto good." |
| Luke 23:34 | Jesus on the Cross: "Father, forgive them; for they know not what they do." |

135

Acts 7:60   Stephen being
                 stoned: "Lord, lay
                 not this sin to their
                 charge."